ABOVE: The frontispiece to Voltaire's Elémens de la Philosophie de Neuton (published in Amsterdam in 1738) depicts Du Châtelet holding a mirror to reflect the light of inspiration from Newton down to the author Voltaire.

First published 2023
This edition © Wooden Books Ltd 2023

Published by Wooden Books Ltd.
Glastonbury, Somerset
www.woodenbooks.com

British Library Cataloguing in Publication Data
Thompson, A.
Daydreams & Thought Experiments

A CIP catalogue record for this book
may be obtained from the British Library

ISBN-10: 1-907155-55-4
ISBN-13: 978-1-907155-55-0

Designed and typeset in Glastonbury, UK.

Printed in China on FSC® certified papers by
RR Donnelley Asia Printing Solutions Ltd.

DAYDREAMS
& THOUGHT EXPERIMENTS

Alec Thompson

To Julia, without whom this book never would have been written

Suggested Reading: *Reasons and Persons*, Derek Parfitt; *Parmenides*, Plato; *A Theory of Justice*, John Rawls; *Thought Experiments*, Nenad Miščević; *Ficciones*, Jorge Luis Borges; *The Dictionary of Obscure Sorrows*, John Koenig; *Essays in Idleness*, Yoshida Kenkō; *The Secret Life of Walter Mitty*, James Thurber; *101 Experiments in the Philosophy of Everyday Life*, Roger-Pol Droit.

ABOVE: The Library of Babel. Argentinian writer Jorge Luis Borges [1899 – 1986] had many incredible daydreams. In one, he imagined a vast library containing books with every possible permutation of letters. This 'Library of Babel' houses every book ever written, and indeed, every book which possibly could be written.

CONTENTS

Introduction   1
The Imagination   2
Daydreams   4
  Humdrum Daydreams   6
  Escapist Daydreams   8
  Disaster Daydreams   10
  Daydreaming the Arts   12
  Guided Daydreams   14
  Mindful Daydreams   16
  Stoic Daydreams   18
  The Ring of Gyges   20
  The Trolley Dilemma   22
  The Original Position   24
  The Experience Machine   26
  Identity Daydreams   28
Thought Experiments   30
  Gaining Knowledge   32
  Paradox   34
  The Ship of Theseus   36
  Self-referential Paradoxes 38
  Newcomb's Paradox   40
  Zeno's Paradox   42
  The Chinese Room   44
  Knowing & Experience   46
  Galileo & Newton   48
  Einstein's Imagination   50
  Schrödinger's cat   52
  Wheeler's Choices   54
  Susskind's Elephant   56
What can be Known   58

ABOVE: A child daydreams about the passage of time. Boëtius Adamsz, c. 1625.
The English, Swedish and Danish word for a daydream is a portmanteau of 'day' and
'dream'. In Czeck, Italian and German, daydreamers are those who dream or sleep with
'open eyes'. These phrases capture the semi-conscious nature of the daydream: you are
not asleep, but neither are you always in full control of what you see.

INTRODUCTION

A T FIRST GLANCE, the two subjects of this book seem like an odd pair. Daydreams are a casual and undisciplined pastime, stereotypically carried out by idlers and airheads. Thought experiments on the other hand are serious and refined creations—they answer Big Questions and are used by scientists and philosophers. Yet, in these pages I will show how the two activities are not so different after all.

We daydream of many things which philosophers also ponder, and the methods of one are similar to those of the other. In fact, the difficulty of drawing a clean line between them is one of the most wondrous things about the pair. To treat them as contiguous is to suggest the world we drift along in daydreams—the surface of our thoughts—and the deep world of the universe explored by thought experiments is somehow connected.

Using only discipline and technique, the daydreamer can dive below and discover a variety of fascinating things: virtue, logic, and justice; personal identity and access to the divine, even the fundamental laws of the universe and the true secrets of morality. And they can do so anywhere: waiting for a train, lying in a field, dozing on the beach or sneakily at the office when the boss isn't looking.

This book will provide the reader with numerous thought experiments, exercises and techniques so that they can carry out these investigations themselves. Virtually everyone daydreams now and then, just as everyone has their own style of fantasy and their own classics and favourites.

All that is required is some free time and a relaxed mind.

THE IMAGINATION
a dream within a dream

Both thought experiments and daydreams are impossible without the imagination, the ability to create something in our minds we are not immediately perceiving. This can be spontaneous, triggered by an object or smell, or it can be deliberate, following an instruction, or completing some task. It can be totally absorbing, occupying all of our attention, as in meditation, or something we run in the 'background', for example when reading a novel. Thought experiments tend to require constrained imagination, while daydreams are more free.

Almost tautologically, anything conceivable can be imagined: impossible shapes and spaces, incredible monsters and ideas for fantastic projects, designs and plans. Equally, imagination makes day-to-day perception and basic communication possible. We can imagine what lies behind objects, retrace and locate hidden things, and anticipate the behaviour of physical systems. We use imagination to read others' minds, imagining what it is like to be them and 'simulating' their likely actions, motives, intentions and mental imagery. Without the telepathy of imagination, ambiguity in language would make communication almost impossible.

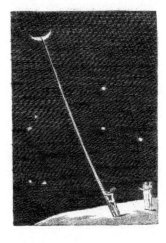

FACING PAGE: The imaginative daydream plays a huge role in human development. Many human actions are preconceived before they are enacted. Engraving by William Blake [1757 – 1827].

LEFT: The suspension of disbelief. All human fiction, from books to movies, involves a narratee entering into a guided daydream.

BELOW: Detail from the Lascaux cave paintings, France, c.15,000BC. The earliest figurative cave painters must have employed some form of daydream to draw in their dark caves. Whether they are shamanic, spells or just images of past or future hunts they all required the painter to imagine something from thin air.

DAYDREAMS
a short history

Daydreaming, like all human activities, has a history. Despite the intensely subjective, private nature of daydreaming, we can identify a few famous historical dreamers. Leonardo da Vinci [1452–1519] was a master, producing ideas ranging from robotic knights to the parachute and helicopter (*opposite top left*). Medieval monks daydreamed of snails fighting knights in the marginalia of manuscripts (*opposite top right*) and Onfim, a 13th century Russian boy, scribbled his daydreams of being a fierce warrior on pieces of bark (*below*).

Daydreaming is not a clearly defined practice. A variety of phrases describe it: Having one's head in the clouds; Being away with the faeries; Mind-wandering; Fantasising; Being lost in reverie; Spontaneous thought; Idle dreaming. The practice of daydreaming is nevertheless widespread and there are many regional variants of daydreamers. There is the German *luftmensch*, Parisian *flaneur* and English *airhead*; further north one can fall into a Scottish *dwam*, and in Japan you get on the *image train* (イメトレ). What these descriptions typically have in common is an emphasis on the carelessness, lack of direction, and drifting of the daydream. Closely connected is the historical suspicion of daydreaming as a time-wasting, utterly unproductive activity reserved for spare moments.

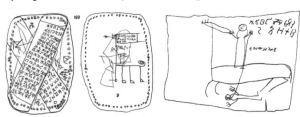

ABOVE: Leonardo da Vinci's "aerial screw", which he drew in the 1480s. Like many new inventions, this will have started as a daydream and then progressed to the conscious imagination.

ABOVE: English medieval manuscripts often show knights fighting snails, a motif that may symbolize either the sin of sloth or the virtue of perseverance.

ABOVE: LEFT: Nightdreams can become daydreams. In the 288 BC Greek Argonautica, Medea experiences elaborate dreams of her future with Jason. RIGHT: What is reality? In the 3rd century BC Chinese Zhuangzi, Zhuang Zho dreams of being a butterfly, but on waking is not sure if he is a man dreaming he is a butterfly, or a butterfly dreaming he is a man.

HUMDRUM DAYDREAMS
problem solved

Waiting for the bus, peeling potatoes, eating a meal alone—daily life rarely takes up 100% of our attention. What do you think about in these moments? A universal activity is to think of plans, projects, and tasks. Often this process is idle, in the sense we do not prioritise and instead drift in and out of themes. *What will I eat tonight? How will I finish this painting? What do I need to get done by the weekend?*

Despite the lack of any overarching plan, this kind of hazy deliberation can be extraordinarily useful. We drift off topic—perhaps for days or even weeks—and when we return we find that what was once muddy is now clear. Our subconscious has tidied up our scattered mental worktop without us even realising it.

Or we begin one plan and end up with something totally unexpected. *Where to go on holiday?* turns into *The zoo last summer was special*, and then *The penguins were great—why don't their feet freeze?* It is not uncommon for these random perambulations to generate insights which surprise us, and likely could not have been produced otherwise.

The practice of mind-wandering involves the paradoxically productive nature of thinking diffusely about nothing in particular. Taking a walk is a classic method, or changing the subject of conversation and cycling back to it. It has a flavour of the totally irrational: *Have you tried not thinking about it at all?*

ABOVE: Odd jobs. Many people use daydreaming to keep on top of what needs to be done in their homes. They may notice a problem, then daydream about how to fix it, from getting up on a roof to fix a gutter or a loose tile, to dusting the top of a four poster bed (facing page).

LEFT: Garden jobs. A walk around the flower beds followed by a short daydream can be a very efficient way to find out what needs to be done, and in what order.

BELOW: Passing the bike shed you remember the bicycle has a slow puncture. You daydream about repairing it, and then remember your pump is broken too.

ESCAPIST DAYDREAMS
imagining the best

There are times in the day when we have nothing to do—waiting for a train, lying in bed waiting to fall asleep, sunbathing on a nice day, the list goes on. A common response to this lull in productivity is to start daydreaming. Perhaps unexpectedly, writers have collected numerous daydreams to try out at home in your free time (*opposite*).

One common daydream, dating at least as far back as the 2nd century, is of travel to exotic places for a holiday or adventure, to experience freedom, culture and nature. If you are so minded, you can go back in time to ancient civilisations, explore future worlds as an artefact of their past, or visit favourite fictional worlds. Why not warp space and fly to the moon (*below*) or shrink yourself to the size of a gnat and explore the concrete mega-scape of a train platform?

8

SOUL MATE
You have romantic fantasies about a secret crush or begin to imagine the perfect partner.

ANOTHER TIME & PLACE
You fantasise about living in a different period of time and/or somewhere else in the world.

RAGS TO RICHES
You imagine winning the lottery or receiving a large sum of money from a relative.

BRUSH WITH FAME
You dream about meeting a famous pop star, actor, politician or scientist.

EXOTIC ADVENTURE
You fantasise about exploring far away lands and holidaying in exciting locations.

CHATTING WITH THE DEAD You imagine having conversations with loved ones who have passed away.

AMAZING PROMOTION
You see yourself achieving huge success in your career or in your personal life.

I AM A SUPERHERO
You daydream about having extraordinary superpowers or special abilities.

REACHING NUMBER ONE
You imagine reaching a goal, like graduating university, or running a marathon.

YOUR MAJESTY
You imagine being in a position of power or authority, lesser or greater.

IF ONLY I'D SAID
You replay good or bad conversations or events, but run a different outcome.

DIFFERENT STROKES
You consider alternate life paths or choices you might have made, or fix mistakes.

COMPLETE MASTERY
You dream about becoming brilliant at a skill or hobby like rollerskating or painting.

I AM THEM
You think about being someone else, like a celebrity or a fictional character.

ABOVE: Some **COMMON DAYDREAMS**. Which of the ones listed above have you experienced? This is not a definitive list, as fantasies vary widely—why not write down a list of your own! FACING PAGE: The Florentine artist Filippo Morghen [1730 – 1807] imagined life on the moon.

DISASTER DAYDREAMS
imagining the worst

One familiar daydream noted by John Koenig [1984–] is the DISASTER DAYDREAM, where the dreamer imagines they are the victim of a tragedy (*opposite*). The details of the calamity can vary immensely, but they generally help you to be grateful for what you have. By imagining sudden death you end up valuing being alive all the more. An imagined disaster can also act as a kind of reset or break—all the complexities and pressing commitments of life fall away.

In his 1921 work *The Psychology of Daydreaming*, J. Varendonck [1879–1924] argues that daydreaming acts as a 'safety-valve' for repressed feelings which otherwise cannot be expressed. Varendonck believed daydreams were not fully conscious or unconscious, nor were they always healthy.

Most 20th century academic commentary followed this critical approach, treating daydreams as a form of neurotic wish-fulfilment with the potential to distract dreamers from reality.

Some authorities still classify daydreaming as a mental disorder. A medical condition called MALADAPTIVE DAYDREAMING diagnoses it as a form of addiction, and involuntary daydreams can be categorised as 'intrusive thoughts.'

OVER THE EDGE
You imagine falling off a cliff, knowing each second is your last. Or you daydream you trip and fall down some stairs.

TRAFFIC ACCIDENT
You are waiting to cross the road and cars zoom past. You imagine what would happen if you took a single step forward.

WHAT IF I WAS GONE
You imagine the world without you. Would anyone care? Would it make a difference? What would you miss?

ILLNESS
You imagine being stricken with disease, lying in hospital. Everything is straightforward—you only need to live.

PLANE CRASH
You are reclining in your seat and daydream a crash. 'Would I survive? If I did, what would I do to reach civilization?'

LOST PHONE
You have lost your mobile phone. Immediately, you imagine how you survive this, and how life might change.

APOCALYPSE
You dream of zombies, plague, an asteroid. Society collapses. What would I do? Where do I find shelter, food and water?

LEFT: An extreme DISASTER DAYDREAM as imagined by Italian painter Achille Beltrame [1871–1945].

FACING PAGE: The Sleep of Reason Produces Monsters, aquatint by Francisco Goya [1746–1828], who wrote of it: "Imagination abandoned by reason produces impossible monsters; united with her, she is the mother of the arts and source of their wonders". The bats are symbols of ignorance, the owls represent folly.

DAYDREAMING THE ARTS
shall we play a game?

Sigmund Freud [1856–1939] suggested some dreamers—artists—can turn their daydreams into forms which appeal to others. Writers can capture the wandering mind's stream of consciousness in words, on paper. Painters have moved back and forth between strict representation and the world of symbol, memory, reverie and dreams. Film is even more effective—the viewer can be made to feel like they are seeing the inside of the characters' minds, an unmediated slideshow of unstructured desires, memories and visions.

We all have ideas for stories, paintings and movies, but most of these only appeal to ourselves, as they stem from our personal foibles, idiosyncrasies, histories and obsessions. The artist, however, can convert their daydreams into something which transcends these limits. Art is the combination of a compelling inner world, and the refined techniques which translate it into something comprehensible to others.

Daydreaming is also used to enjoy art. Art triggers the imagination, providing a structure for the make-believe world. Once we enter this world, and get lost in some art, or a daydream, what is true and false changes; our responses, attitudes, and beliefs may alter radically, and we will be carried along until our suspension of disbelief is broken.

ABOVE: LEFT: Winsor McCay was an early 20th century illustrator who used his vivid daydreams to create fantastical and surreal worlds. RIGHT: Dream psyche image, c. 1920, by the psychologist Carl Jung, reminiscent of alchemical or aboriginal works of art.

ACTIVE PSYCHE
pleasure seeking

ACTIVE STATE
paintball gaming
impulse buying

full immersion in
REAL WORLD
inner and outer

WILLING
SUSPENSION OF
DISBELIEF

MEDIUM STATE
video/board games
kids play games

PASSIVE PSYCHE
desire to escape

PASSIVE STATE
full immersion in
books, plays, movies

ABOVE: THE SUSPENSION OF DISBELIEF occurs when a person enters into a work of fiction, a picture or a game, and willingly forgets the make-believe nature of this new world.

FACING PAGE. In his 1947 novel The Secret Life of Walter Mitty, author James Thurber contrasts the hero's mundane life with the adventures he imagines himself in. His constant daydreaming leads to problems in relationships and his ability to function in the real world.

GUIDED DAYDREAMS
the power of imagination

The brain sometimes finds it difficult to distinguish between imagined and real experiences and can respond as strongly to an imagined situation as it would to a real one. Guided visualizations use this effect as a therapeutic tool to rewire our experience of the world.

Stepping back from daily life and imagining a peaceful scene releases tension, leading to decreased heart rate and blood pressure (*below*). Focused visualizations can bring a fresh perspective to problems and assist in overcoming any limiting beliefs (*opposite*). Furthermore, creating a vivid mental picture visualizing yourself achieving your goals can help identify the steps that make your dreams a reality.

7-STEP STRESS-REDUCING
MEDITATION.

1. *Imagine standing on a beautiful beach.* 2. *Feel the breeze on your skin and the sand beneath your feet.* 3. *Hear the waves on the shore and smell the salty air.* 4. *Exhale, letting go of any tension.* 5. *Walk to the sea and enjoy it washing over your toes and ankles.* 6. *Walk deeper until the water reaches your waist.* 7. *Feel the gentle sway of the waves and let yourself be completely present in this bountiful moment of peace.*

Night on the Shores of Lake Ilmen, Ivan Bilibin, 1913.

HEALING LIGHT
Work up your body, from toes to head, imagining each part infused with light.

GROWING NATURALLY
Picture flowers, plants and trees to symbolize growth and personal development.

STEP BY STEP
Imagine small positive changes, to help prepare for when opportunities arise.

AT HOME
Imagine the self as a house. Explore each of the rooms, staircases, cellars and attic.

DISTANCING PHOBIA
Imagine seeing yourself watching a feared situation on a screen, to overcome fear.

VOYAGING
Visualize the steps of a journey to represent travelling towards a goal.

LEFT: GUIDED QUESTIONS MEDITATION.

1. Close your eyes and relax. Imagine that you are in a forest. Describe the forest. 2. You see a path. What do you do? 3. You come to a lake. Describe the lake. 4. What do you do? 5. You see a house. What does it look like? 6. Is there anyone there? 7. Do you go in the house?

The forest represents your attitude to life, the lake represents your attitude to sexuality, and the house represents your attitude to death.

Sacred Grove, Toshi Yoshida, woodblock print, 1941.

Mindful Daydreams
visualising oneness

MEDITATION interacts with daydreaming in fascinating ways. One interesting exercise is to contemplate zen *koans*, paradoxical riddles designed to induce enlightenment (*opposite*). Another is *zazen*, essentially sitting down and letting the mind wander without dwelling on any thoughts in particular. A useful metaphor is cloud watching: thoughts are treated as drifting clouds, witnessed but not fixated upon.

Neuroscience suggests that letting the mind wander can be beneficial as it uses the *default mode network*, a background brain process which is always active though not always conscious. Strengthening this network can help you form unlikely connections between ideas, think more diffusely about the past and present, and improve your creativity.

MINDFULNESS is a similar practice which emphasises the present moment and non-judgement. To practice, exclude everyday noise and concentrate on bodily processes such as breathing and taste; if distracted, neutrally acknowledge the drift before returning to your initial focus.

Buddhists, who created many of these techniques, say that mindfulness allows us to ignore the transient desires of the world, become more spiritually conscious and find the path to enlightenment. A more recent trend treats it as a health practice, like exercise or dieting. Improvements are said to include stress reduction, increased concentration, better sleep, and chronic pain management.

ONE HAND CLAPPING
When two hands clap there is a sound.
What is the sound of one hand?

UMMON IS ASKED
"What teaching transcends the Buddha and
patriarchs?" Ummon said, "A sesame bun."

THE MIND OF DOG
Has a dog Buddha-nature? This is the most
serious question of all. If you say yes or no,
you lose your own Buddha-nature.

THE GIRL
Seijo had two souls, one always sick at home
and the other in the city, a married woman
with two children. Which was the true soul?

YOUR ORIGINAL FACE
What is your original face before you were
born? Show me your original face before your
mother and father were born.

TWO MONKS AND A FLAG
One says, "The flag is moving." The other,
"The wind is moving." A third says, "Not the
wind, not the flag; the mind is moving."

STOIC DAYDREAMS
virtue, ethics & impermanence

What of the relationship between daydreaming and ethics? One school of ancient Greek philosophers, the Stoics, believed daydreaming was an essential part of living a virtuous life, and that one's attitude towards events was more important than the outcome. Two Stoics, Marcus Aurelius and Seneca, argued that the height of virtue was to treat tragedy and success with equanimity. In doing so, the stoic sage can retain their integrity regardless of misfortune.

A core part of Stoicism is the practice and living of these ideals: *askēsis*. Each day, the practitioner imagines all the awful things which could occur and then waits for the anxiety, sadness, and fear to pass before reflecting: *These terrible events may affect my body, family, possessions, but they cannot affect my attitude and my mind. I remain in control of these and no bandit, typhoon or fire can deprive me of them.*

Numerous exercises help to achieve this mentality—remembering and accepting mortality; reflecting on the impermanence of possessions and achievements; contextualising the importance or triviality of events and feelings in life's broader picture. For the Stoic, daydreaming is a meaningful process: you must not become attached to your visions, whether in avarice, longing, fear or obsession, but rather learn detachment and control. By mastering the inner world, we master our reactions to external events and, in so doing, become virtuous.

KISSING GOODNIGHT
When you kiss your kids goodnight or your friends goodbye, always remember it may be the last time you ever see each other.

ALL BORROWED
To help loosen your attachment to things remember that everything you have is only borrowed, temporarily.

THAT ANNOYED ME
Know your own faults, for faults you find in another are often your own. See every day as a training exercise, with scratches.

STAY IN THE PRESENT
The past and future are not under our control, so why worry about them? Better to focus on the task at hand, which is this moment, now.

SWAP SHOES
When dealing with people, put yourself in their shoes, to see their perspective. This will help you do good, not only no evil.

COUNT BLESSINGS
At all times, always remember how lucky you are to have what you have, rather than focusing on what you don't have.

YOUR REACTION
You have no control over other people, or events. The only thing you can control is your reaction to them. So imagine your best reactions.

PART OF A WHOLE
Visualise friends and enemies as limbs and organs of a larger body. We are all brothers and sisters, part of a single living being.

FACING PAGE: **MEMENTO MORI**, Stoic visual aids used to "remember death": Skulls: the inevitability of death. Hourglasses: the passage of time. Candles: the fleeting nature of life. Flowers: the impermanence of beauty. Moths: the brevity of life.

ABOVE: Examples of Stoic daydreaming exercises. For example, whenever you look at a clock, remember to be in the present. Whenever you look at someone's shoes, put yourself in them. Whenever you see a mirror, remember that the world reflects you back.

The Ring of Gyges

take the precious, yes

In his *Republic*, Plato asks us to imagine finding a magic ring which renders its wearer invisible. In his allegory, a shepherd uses such a ring to sneak into the palace, seduce the queen, murder the king and steal the crown. The question Plato asks, via his dialogue with Glaucon, is could anyone resist wrongdoing wearing such a ring?

Glaucon posits two men finding such rings: one moral, the other immoral. He argues that the good man would inevitably succumb to temptation and act wickedly. So, when consequences and social scrutiny are stripped away, the good man is equivalent to the bad, and thus 'good' behaviour is mostly due to fear of social or legal repercussion. Socrates' replies that the doer of evil deeds, whilst free of social bonds, is enslaved to his own passions. In contrast, he who stays good follows his inner rationality, and is thus free and happy.

Let us consider two inversions of this allegory (*opposite top*). The first is to ask how many of your good deeds were done out of a desire for social approval. What is the kindest act you would do without anyone knowing about it? Paradoxically, perhaps true goodness—good done for its own sake—is only possible with the ring on. The second is more disturbing: what if your sins are not prevented but in fact *caused* by social pressure to carry out evil acts: for example, in Nazi Germany or in some world where living a law-abiding life is certain to produce injustice. In these worlds, the Ring of Gyges's power is inverted: it becomes liberating rather than enslaving.

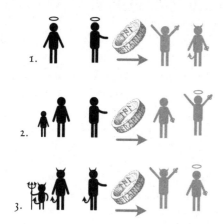

1. The ring provides impunity and, free of constraint, people become corrupted. This instance assumes a situational morality where people are only good because of a fear of the consequences.

2. Is kindness driven solely by reward? Perhaps truly selfless acts, with no expectation of praise or gain, reflect the purest form of goodness.

3. When society itself is wicked, the ring becomes a symbol of empowerment. It allows us to subvert established power structures and create positive change free from external pressures.

ABOVE: LEFT: The Invisible Man. CENTRE: Dr Jekyll / Mr Hyde. Both choose to use the Ring of Gyges for evil (albeit in different guises). The former becomes a dictator, the latter a murderous brute. The stories relate Victorian hypocrisy and obsession with virtue to Glaucon's argument that good and bad people are equivalent when no-one is looking. RIGHT: Gollum, by M. Belomlinskij. Tolkien's 1954 epic The Lord of the Rings can be viewed as essentially a long meditation on whether or not to use the Ring of Gyges, and the plentiful hazards that emerge from doing so.

THE TROLLEY DILEMMA
tracks & snacks

Imagine a train hurtling down the tracks towards three helpless people. There is a solution: you can pull a lever and redirect the train so that it switches track, crushing only one. What do you do?

This dilemma, known as the TROLLEY PROBLEM, can be used to test a variety of intuitions (*opposite*). The experimenter can investigate the moral relevance of the number of people: if three seems difficult, try a thousand, or something inconceivable like five trillion. They can explore the relevance of the victims' characteristics: for instance, by specifying that the three are all old, whereas the singleton is a baby. Or their moral desert: it might be a choice between three murderers and one innocent, or three brilliant scientists with a cure for cancer and an average joe. Maybe it is personal and the single one is your mother or child. Do these affect how eager you are to pull that lever?

Alternatively, you could change the scenario: for instance, the default is such that the train will crush the single person without your intervention. Or that instead of a lever you must stop the train, saving the three, by pushing someone else onto the tracks—would you do it? Could you? These problems have increasingly been crawling out of philosophers' brains into the real world. Take the autonomous car (*right*): how should we programme it to react when the options are 1. killing a pedestrian, or 2. killing the driver?

I.

2.

THE TROLLEY PROBLEM

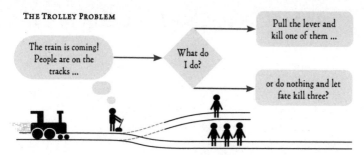

The train is coming! People are on the tracks ...

What do I do?

Pull the lever and kill one of them ...

or do nothing and let fate kill three?

ABOVE: In 2003 a real life runaway train was hurtling towards another waiting at a station. Diverting it would derail it into a poor area of housing, but the operators decided to anyway. Miraculously, no-one was killed, but several houses were destroyed. Very few trolley problems are purely about ethics, they also involve politics and who gets to pull the lever.

THE HUNGRY PROBLEM

Shiver me timbers! We've run out of food

What do I do?

I could eat a shipmate and I would survive

or I could let my shipmates eat me ...

or I can refuse to eat, and hope for rescue

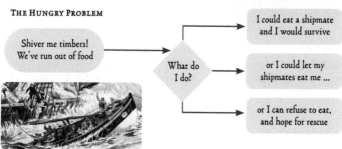

ABOVE: The Mignonette set sail in 1884 with a crew of four but only arrived with two. The ship was caught in a storm and the crew forced into a lifeboat. Running out of food, the crew voted on who to eat to feed the rest. They decided it should be Parker, the orphan cabin boy, on the basis the others had families. They killed and ate Parker who allegedly said 'What, me?' before his death. They were charged and found guilty of murder. What would you do?

THE ORIGINAL POSITION
let them eat cake

You are chosen to cut a birthday cake at a party: how do you decide the size of a slice? Is it by merit, age, height, belief or wealth?

John Rawls [1921–2002] called these questions problems of *distributive justice* and tried to create the perfect unbiased procedure for deciding them. His answer was the *original position*. Participants imagine they have entered a state of being where they forget their place in society: their wealth, age, skill, health, religion, gender, race, job and class. Instead, they are blinded by a 'veil of ignorance'—they could be anyone, anywhere. Rawls investigates how someone stripped of all personal knowledge would divide the resources of society. How would you?

Rawls argued the most logical response is equality: after all, you have no idea who you will be when the veil is lifted, how old, tall, wealthy, etc, so it makes sense to cut equal slices (*opposite centre*).

What makes this puzzling is that the premises seem reasonable but lead to a radical conclusion. Do you accept this way of deciding society's distributive scheme? And if not, what it is you find unfair? When considering who gets what, does wealth matter to you? Does religion? How committed are you to equal concern and respect for all? The genius behind the original position is that it forces us to reconcile intuitions which, though contradictory, are usually left unquestioned.

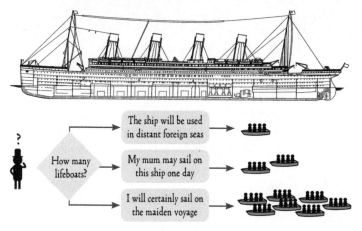

ABOVE: LIFEBOATS. *You are commissioning a new ship and have a choice in how much you spend on lifeboats. Would your choice be different if you did not know if you will be on board?*

RIGHT: *Who cuts the cake? Or perhaps we should say that the person who cuts chooses the slice last. Rawls has been influential and popular because of the intuitiveness of using a fair procedure to get a fair result.*

LEFT: *Another example of procedural justice is in the form of 'eeny meeny miny mo, catch a tiger by the toe...' where the seeming incontrovertibly of a fair procedure suggests objectivity of some kind.*

FACING PAGE: *Could the 'veil of ignorance' be applied to nationality? If so, this would lead to the conclusion that rich countries are under a duty to transfer wealth and assist poorer ones.*

THE EXPERIENCE MACHINE
a glitch in the matrix

What is the role of 'reality' in living an ethical and meaningful life? Imagine you are playing piano at a party (*below*): does it matter if the piano, your friends, the room, even the birthday cake are part of an artificial simulation? This is a thought experiment created by philosopher Robert Nozick [1938–2002], who imagined the *experience machine*, a device capable of simulating any sensation whatsoever.

Once ensconced in the experience machine the user can feel the thrill of a scientific breakthrough, the taste of a world-class meal, or the joy of love, all at the push of a button. The device can create a perfectly flourishing existence. Or can it? Nozick's experiment is designed to raise doubts about how satisfying such a life would be. Is the sensation enough or do we actually want to live it? What about you? Could you be satisfied with the experience of pure pleasure, or do you need something more for a fulfilling life?

Consider the opposite of the experience machine: you are not given the option to plug-in, you are given the option to plug-out: you are in the machine right now! Your daily life today is entirely false, generated by the experience machine and fed to your sleeping body. The twist, however, is that the real world is empty, devoid of pleasure and other people. Nonetheless, it is real. Would you unplug, even if it meant 'dying' in the simulation and leaving your family and friends behind?

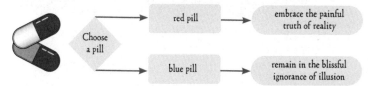

```
                    red pill  ───────►  embrace the painful
                                         truth of reality
Choose
a pill
                    blue pill ───────►  remain in the blissful
                                         ignorance of illusion
```

ABOVE: **MORPHEUS' CHOICE**: *In the film The Matrix, the protagonist Neo must choose either a red pill or a blue pill. If he takes the red, he will awaken to the painful truth that he is in a vegetative state, living in a simulation. If he chooses blue, he can remain blissfully unaware.*

LEFT: **THE CAVE**. *in The Republic, c.375 BC, Plato uses the Allegory of the Cave to contrast sensory information and knowledge obtained by reason. Prisoners are chained up in a cave believing that shadows cast on the wall are the only reality. One is freed (educated), experiences the outside world, and returns to enlighten the others. But they think he has gone mad, and prefer to believe in their shadows. 'Falling in love with the lie', they deny the truth when told of the falsity of their existence.*

FACING PAGE: **THE EXPERIENCE MACHINE**. *1. Do we want to actually be a world-class pianist, or 2. is it enough to experience the sensation of what it is like to be one?*

27

IDENTITY DAYDREAMS
and Parfitt's puzzles

Daydreaming is an excellent way to explore one's identity. Relax, and consider these visualisations designed to test aspects of personality.

1. ADDITION AND SUBTRACTION: popularised by psychotherapy, this exercise tests which parts of identity are central to the concept of self. Imagine an emotionally charged situation, like being embarrassed in public or a lottery win. Then gradually change small elements of your personality—favourite colour, age, hair style, before changing more radical things like religion, sexuality, gender, and race (*below*). When do you cease identifying with this person? On reaching this point, add or subtract elements to determine what exactly makes you 'you'.

2. FIRST AND SECOND: this exercise is drawn from moral philosophy and helps clarify the nature of desire. It works on the premise there are two kinds: first-order desires are straightforward attractions to things: money, affection, objects, adventure. Second-order desires are the desire (or non-desire) for first-order desires. The two frequently come apart: *I may want to smoke but don't want the habit* or *I may be a homebody but wish I was more adventurous*. The exercise asks two questions: (a) *Of all present desires, which is my favourite?* and (b) *Of the desires I see in others, which would I want?* Although simple, these questions can be difficult to answer, and even more difficult to put into practice.

1.

2.

28

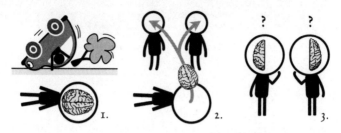

ABOVE: **THE CRASH**: *This puzzle explores partial physical continuity. 1. You are in a crash and die. 2. Your brain is split and transplanted into two separate brainless bodies. 3. Each has your subjective memories, tendencies, idiosyncrasies and believes they are you, so what happened to 'you'? If only half your brain had survived, you wouldn't be considered dead, so why does it matter if both halves are transplanted? Perhaps there are two of you, but are they both the 'same person'? Questions of identity were a speciality of Derek Parfitt [1942–2017].*

ABOVE: **THE TELETRANSPORT PARADOX**: *1. Travelling in a spaceship you use a teleporter, which 2. scans and destroys the 'you' inside to create an duplicate 'you' on a nearby planet. But is this duplicate really you? 3. Say the teleporter malfunctioned and 4. didn't destroy the original, are there now two of you? If the duplicate is not 'you', then perhaps mental and physical continuity are necessary for identity to persist and the body's destruction results in death. Parfitt noted that although this may seem a solution, it only opens the door to new difficulties.*

THOUGHT EXPERIMENTS
an introduction

A *thought experiment* is an imagined scenario designed to answer a particular question. The experimenter may want to discover facts, such as the movement of objects, the laws of light, or the rules of the quantum. Conversely, they may seek truths of a different kind: the quality of justice; what it is to be ethical; the requirements of logic.

The methodologies of thought experiments and physical experiments are similar. The experimenter sets up a series of objects in a scenario and observes how they interact. At first glance there seems a fundamental difference between an imagined experiment and a real one—the former is entirely within the mind of the experimenter. However, in both cases the experimenter does not always know how the experiment will turn out. The experimental scenario may be imaginary, but frequently its execution produces a feeling of discovering something new. The conclusions of thought experiments can be deeply counterintuitive and thus unlikely to be reached outside the constructed scenario.

Also, like physical experiments, thought experiments are often subsequently modified to refine the original findings and produce new discoveries. In this way, a thought experiment can occasionally transcend the original mind which developed it. Finally, both thought experiments and their physical cousins require discipline to keep all the variables under control. Only then can they discover the fundamental truths they are seeking.

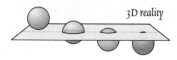

3D reality

2D flatlander view

time

LEFT: In **FLATLAND**, the 1884 novella by Edwin Abbott, we follow a square's journey through different dimensions. The 2D inhabitants of Flatland are unable to perceive the existence of a third dimension, leading to misunderstanding and conflict when they interact with a 3D reality. The tale highlights the limitations of perception and the need to consider multiple perspectives in order to fully comprehend the world.

RIGHT: **MAXWELL'S DEMON** was proposed by James Clerk Maxwell [1831–1879] as a test of the second law of thermodynamics.

1. A demon cunningly controls a gate so that fast molecules pass to one side of a box and slow molecules to the other, sorting the box.

2. Since temperature depends on velocity, one side warms and the other cools, decreasing the system's total entropy thus violating the second law, which is deemed impossible!

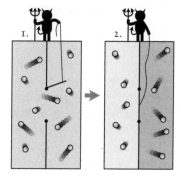

LEFT: **LAPLACE'S DEMON**. In 1814 Pierre-Simon Laplace posited that according to causal determinism, if a demon knew the location and momentum of every atom in the universe, all past and future values could be calculated. We now know this is impossible. E.g. There are irreversible thermodynamical processes where past positions and momenta simply cannot be reconstructed.

GAINING KNOWLEDGE
epistemology & thought experiments

Epistemology is the study of knowledge, in particular, the nature of knowledge as opposed to belief or opinion. Whether or not thought experiments can provide knowledge is intensely debated. Science relies on repeated experimental evidence, and merely thinking seems to bypass this laborious process. However, thought experiments do seem to have advanced scientific knowledge, so what is going on?

The thought experiment could be a hypothesis predicting how the world will work informed by past experience, to be confirmed by experiment. But such predictions use expectations arising from experience and, problematically, many thought experiments cannot be easily reformulated in terms of deductions from existing laws of nature, especially when using an unusual invented scenario.

Or maybe thought experiments access *a priori* truths, which exist outside and before empirical data, like a mathematician deriving results from first principles? However, not all thought experiments are reliable: some are built on shaky suppositions and it is not clear how to identify which are *a priori* truths outside testing them by experiment.

Perhaps thought experiments involve *mental models*—a visual, spatial picture of how the world works built using past experience, like *Objects fall when dropped*. This means that sometimes it can reveal intuitions that could not have articulated or consciously explained. As a result, the mental model can give the impression of providing new knowledge when these implicit intuitions are manipulated and combined. But even so, are any these intuitions themselves *a priori*, i.e. which thought experiments need to be tested by real experiments?

RIGHT: **THE EPITAPH OF STEVINUS.**
A thought experiment posed by early scientist
Simon Stevin [1548 – 1620] proves the
mechanical advantage of inclined planes. It
shows that a special arrangement of beads
placed on a frictionless plane must be static,
otherwise there would be perpetual motion.

LEFT: **DESCARTES' METHOD OF DOUBT.**
Associated with René Descartes [1596 –
1650], Cartesian doubt involves imagining
that everything you believe is false in order to
be certain of that which is true. Seen by many
as the root of the modern scientific method,
it forms the basis for Descartes' statement,
"Cogito ergo sum" (I think, therefore I am).

RIGHT: **THE PROBLEM OF INDUCTION.**
Formulated by David Hume [1711 – 1776],
this philosophical problem questions whether
past experience is a reliable guide to predicting
future events. It argues that there is no justified
way of making inferences from the observed
to the unobserved, raising concerns about how
we can know anything with certainty.

LEFT: **THE GETTIER PROBLEM.**
Mr Jones thinks he sees his cow in a field,
unaware that it is actually a replica cow
placed as a prank. In a twist of fate, however,
his real cow is hiding behind the fake. Does
Mr Jones know if there is a cow in the field?
Attributed to Edmund Gettier [1927 – 2021],
the problem suggests that it is possible to have
a justified true belief that is not knowledge.

PARADOX
this can't be right

A good example of a thought experiment is the *paradox*. There are many kinds, but the most devastating are those which reveal how two seemingly obvious intuitions must in fact be incompatible.

One of the oldest is the SORITES PARADOX. Imagine a heap of 1,000,000 grains of wheat. Removing one makes no difference: 999,999 grains is still a heap. Repeating the process, however, eventually leaves us with the nonsensical conclusion that a single grain is a heap (*opposite top*), as removing one grain is immaterial to the 'heapness' of the pile. A solution is to define a point where it ceases to be a heap: say 5,000 grains. But is it really the case that 5,000 grains is a heap whereas 4,999 is not?

Now consider two related paradoxes. The first is the infamous LIAR'S PARADOX: the sentence *This sentence is false*. If true then it must therefore be false; if it is false it must therefore be true!

RUSSELL'S PARADOX is a similar idea that relates to the mathematical concept of the *set*—a collection of things, such as people, numbers, and also other sets; i.e. the set of red things includes fire engines, strawberries, and red pens. Now imagine the 'set of all sets which do not contain themselves as members' (S). Does this set contain itself? If so, then it cannot be a member, for the set only contains sets which do not contain themselves (*right*). But if it doesn't contain itself then it is a 'set which does not contain itself' and must be part of the set! The repercussions of this paradox for set theory were huge and shaped mathematical history.

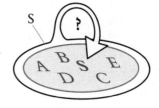

34

A HEAP

A HEAP?

NOT A HEAP

Unnameable

FAR LEFT: THE PINOCCHIO PARADOX
When Pinocchio says "Now my nose grows!", will it grow or not, as his nose will only grow when he is lying?

NEAR LEFT: BHARTRHARI'S paradox:
Nothing can be unnameable or unsignifiable, as this results in that thing being called 'unnameable'.

RIGHT: THE PARADOX OF THE COURT:
The Sophist Protagoras took on a new pupil, Euathlus; the tuition fees would be paid after his first court win. But Euathlus decided not to become a lawyer, so Protagoras sued him, reasoning: If I win, then the court will order him to pay me, but if Euathlus wins, then he has won his first case and will have to pay me.

If I win, he pays me!

If I lose, he pays me!

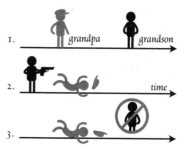

1.   grandpa   grandson

2.   time

3.

LEFT: The GRANDFATHER PARADOX:
A time traveller goes back in time to kill his grandfather. If he succeeds, his father can't be born, thus the time traveller would not exist to kill the grandfather. Yet if the grandfather lives, then the time traveller could carry out the assassination. Paradoxically, it seems the time traveller both can and cannot kill his grandfather.

THE SHIP OF THESEUS
the same but different

King Theseus has a favourite ship. Due to wear and tear, beams, planks and fittings are occasionally replaced. One day, he realises not a single piece of the original ship remains. In a rage, he shouts This isn't my ship! and burns it. So, does his reaction make sense? Or was the incinerated ship the same as the one he started with?

Now let's change the scenario—what if Queen Phaedra secretly kept the planks the King threw away and rebuilt the ship in secret. There would be two ships, but which would be *the* ship of Theseus?

What of human beings, who also change over time? Is a 99-year-old is the same as the ten-year-old she once was when no actual cell is shared between them? Perhaps she is the same person because she has the same memories, feelings, reactions. Would your answer change if she suffered a brain injury and lost all her memories, including a radical shift in personality? How many memories and characteristics must she keep: at what point does she 'die' and become someone new?

If these puzzles seem insoluble, you could perhaps argue, like Parfitt, that identity is simply a matter of degree, the 'individual' being akin to Wittgenstein's string, of which no strand runs the whole.

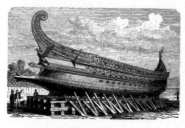

LEFT: THE SHIP OF THESEUS:
If all the parts of an object have been replaced, is it still the original? What if the original parts are reassembled? The puzzle raises questions about the nature of identity and whether an object can maintain its perceptual continuity despite changes.

RIGHT: THE GRAND ISE SHRINE:
Every twenty years the Ise shrine in Japan is burnt to the ground and then entirely rebuilt. The Shinto priests say it is the same shrine that has stood there for two millennia. It is obviously not physically the same building, but is treated as such. Is this reasonable?

LEFT: GETTING OLD:
Is an old lady the same person as she was when young? While the body undergoes constant change, identity is primarily tied to psychological continuity. Brain injury, memory loss, or gradual mental deterioration can all disrupt or challenge our fragile sense of personal identity.

RIGHT: THE ROTATING DOOR
You live in a small town. People come and go, have children, die. This continues for years until no original residents remain. Is it the same town? If not, at what point did it change? What gives the town its identity, and can we ask the same question of larger groups, like companies and countries?

SELF-REFERENTIAL PARADOXES
looking at looking at looking

Many paradoxes arise as a consequence of self-reference: the paradoxical nature of This *sentence is false*, for example, arises from the way it refers to itself (*see page 34*). Self-reference can produce similar issues and quirks within dreams and daydreams. Self-referential night dreams for example—ones which refer to the fact they are a dream— are typically unstable and the dreamer wakes up quickly once she becomes aware. The exception is the lucid dream which can continue indefinitely despite being a dream of dreaming.

Daydreams which reference themselves are more complicated. It may be pleasant to daydream about being someone different doing interesting things in distant places, nonetheless, it is less pleasant to explicitly recognise that it is all fantasy (*opposite top left*).

Unlike the nightdream, there is no lucid daydream. Nevertheless, the daydreamer must not forget they are in a daydream—to do so and mistake fantasy for reality is to become delusional. The daydream is in this sense paradoxical. The daydreamer must simultaneously recognise and deny the unreality of their imagined worlds.

One phrase for this process is *paradoxieentfaltung* which translates as 'the unfolding of paradoxes'. As used by the German sociologist Niklas Luhmann[1927–1998], it describes the way paradox can create meaning. Many institutions are contingent and socially constructed, like money, legality and newsworthiness; however, we treat them as real and immutable. The same can be said of daydreams: we enjoy them as if they are fulfilling experiences whilst remembering they are fantasies and thus within our control to change, manipulate, and erase.

ABOVE: **A Daydream of Daydreaming**:
*Imagine lying in a field daydreaming of
exotic travels. Does it feel satisfying, or is it
better to directly daydream of travelling?*

ABOVE: **DRAWING HANDS**:
*In M.C. Escher's 1948 lithograph, each
'drawer' is, from its own perspective, the
observer, but is in turn observed by the other.*

ABOVE: **DOUBLE MEANINGS**. *René
Magritte's 1929 painting is both a pipe and
an image of a pipe. According to Luhmann,
self reference involves paradox. Observing
an object grants it an independent existence,
whilst recognising meaning requires
observing the distinction. In the first 'mode'
you must forget you are creating the object;
in the second, you must recognise that you
are creating it.* LEFT: *Optical illusions work
in much the same way. Duck/Rabbit and
Man's Head illusion by Sandro del Prete.*

NEWCOMB'S PARADOX
& the acausal control puzzle

Is rational decision-making all that it seems? William Newcomb [1927–1999] came up with a paradox that tests rationality to its limits. Picture two boxes: Box A is clear and has £1000 inside, Box B is opaque and its content is set in advance by a prescient god whose predictions are almost always correct. You may either choose Box B, or both boxes. If the god predicted that you would take box B then it hid £1,000,000 inside (*opposite top*), but if it predicted you would take *both* then it left box B empty. What do you do (*see opposite*)?

In another version of this exercise, you find yourself in a sealed room while far away an exact copy of you is created with all of your memories and characteristics. You both have the same choice: either *cooperate* and send £1,000,000 to your perfect copy's sealed room, or *defect* and receive a £1000 bonus for yourself. Which do you choose? There seems to be no benefit to cooperating—there is no communication so you cannot influence your duplicate and the game is only played once so there is no risk of losing their trust. If sending £1,000,000 has no benefit to you, why not take the £1000 and wait for a potential £1,000,000? The catch is that a truly perfect twin will do the same as you do… in which case you can control your copy's decision in a strange way.

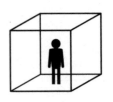
By defecting you ensure they will also defect; on the other hand, simply cooperate and they will too!
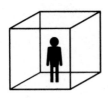

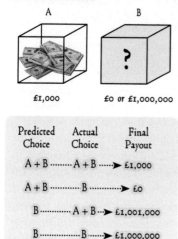

A   B

£1,000   £0 or £1,000,000

Predicted Choice	Actual Choice	Final Payout
A + B	A + B	£1,000
A + B	B	£0
B	A + B	£1,001,000
B	B	£1,000,000

LEFT: In **NEWCOMB'S PARADOX** you must choose only box B or both boxes, A & B. If the almost omniscient god predicted you take only box B, then it will have put £1,000,000 inside, but if it predicted you take both, then you will find B is empty. Maybe you should take both; the god has already filled the boxes and your choice cannot change that. But then you might only get £1000. Do you act rationally and get punished, or irrationally and receive a reward? As Robert Nozick notes: "To almost everyone it is perfectly clear and obvious what should be done. The difficulty is that these people seem to divide almost evenly on the problem, with large numbers thinking that the opposing half is just being silly."

THE PERFECT TWIN PUZZLE

You are in a sealed room, like your clone → cooperate with your clone?

→ yes, send them £1,000,000 → hope they do the same!

→ no, receive £1,000 → hope they did the opposite!

ABOVE: The **PERFECT TWIN PUZZLE**, as philosopher Joe Carlsmith has pointed out, appears to violate the laws of causation – the moment one acts the other acts too, regardless of distance. Time is also irrelevant: it does not matter if the copy exists in the present, past or future. In all cases their behaviour is controlled by the twin. The puzzle relies on a mechanistic understanding of the brain. The contrary position is that there is some degree of randomness: e.g. consciousness may emerge from quantum states in the brain. If so, two identically instantiated brains might collapse their quantum states differently, thus behaving in a non-mechanistic way.

ZENO'S PARADOX
slices of the infinite

Beatrice faces a firing squad. Luckily she is beside the philosopher Zeno, who says not to worry: if they slowly move back the bullet will never reach them. When the bullet reaches where they were, they'll have moved back a little and the bullet has to catch up, however by then they're back further still and so on forever. Beatrice is not totally reassured, but cannot find the flaw in Zeno's reasoning. Can you?

Zeno's paradox raises questions about the infinite division of space and has been affected by scientific developments. Mathematically, it can be shown that an infinite number of increasingly small portions makes a single whole. Consider a magic ship voyaging to a kingdom one kilometre away: every hour it halves the remaining distance it needs to travel. Can it reach the kingdom? The answer is theoretically yes, as an infinite number of successive halves adds up to one (*below*).

What if each halving took a particular amount of time? Say each takes one second; during the first it travels at $\frac{1}{2}$ kms^{-1}, the second at $\frac{1}{4}$ kms^{-1}, the third, $\frac{1}{8}$ kms^{-1} and so on. Since the ship continually slows, the journey would take forever and it would never reach the kingdom. On the other hand, if the time taken to halve the distance also halves, then although there are infinite number of tiny time slices, they add up to a finite time, just as the infinite number of slices of distance add up to a kilometre. Finally, note that at incredibly small distances our ordinary intuitions break down and we enter the quantum realm where the behaviour of objects becomes radically uncertain.

$$\frac{1}{2} + \frac{1}{4} + \frac{1}{8} + \frac{1}{16} + \cdots = \sum_{n=1}^{\infty} \left(\frac{1}{2}\right)^n = 1$$

LEFT: ZENO'S PARADOX:
Achilles is racing a tortoise, which has a head start. Before he catches up with the tortoise, Achilles has to cover half the distance. But when he gets there the tortoise has moved on a bit, and then he to cover half the remaining distance. And so on, ad infinitum. How can he ever reach it?

RIGHT: BORGE'S CLOCK:
Jorge Borges [1899 – 1986] famously asked this question: How do we ever get to midnight? The clock has to reach five minutes to midnight first, then 2.5 minutes to midnight, then 1.25 minutes, and so on—so it seems the clock will never reach midnight! How can we explain this?

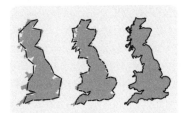

LEFT: THE COASTLINE PARADOX:
How long is the coastline of Great Britain? By increasing the magnification and decreasing the size of the units of measurement, taking in more and more details, the coastline of the UK seems to continue growing in size forever (apart from maybe when it hits the planck length).

RIGHT: The HUMMINGBIRD BRAIN:
Consider someone whose brain runs at the speed of a hummingbird's and every second feels like a hundred. Would they live longer than a normal person even if both die on their 99th birthday? Further, would it be better to choose the hummingbird person over the normal one in a trolley-problem?

THE CHINESE ROOM
can intelligence be artificial?

Bob wants to converse with his friend Yi Jie, but lacks the time to learn Chinese. Instead, he has a book with instructions on which characters to use in response to which (*opposite top*). It works well: the book is so sophisticated that Bob's responses appear to come from an active, intelligent conversation partner. But they aren't, because Bob has no idea what his friend is asking, nor what he is replying. Does Bob 'know' Chinese? The puzzle is intended to show that computation alone is not the same as thought: there is no 'meaning' or understanding behind Bob's responses. On the other hand, perhaps there is: the handbook contains an understanding of Chinese, Bob is just a cog, like the moving lips of a native speaker. The difficulty then is: who, or what, is thinking—isn't Bob just mechanically shuffling symbols to match others, and can it really be said the book 'knows' Chinese?

Stranger still is Ludwig Boltzmann's 1896 idea that there is a nonzero chance that space dust and detritus could randomly form a complete, operating brain (*opposite lower mid*). It is *possible*, over the vast lifetime of the universe. Given infinite time, the number of these brains could outnumber non-Boltzmann brains. Boltzmann went further: whilst the brain may only survive for a moment, there is a chance it could form in such a way as to have complex memories, experiences, and beliefs. The brain would be in the same position as you and I. It wouldn't know if it had just been created, and its past memories all false, or if it had actually lived those memories. It would be very like a 'brain in a vat' experiment (*opposite lower*), where a disembodied brain is fed a complete, simulated experience and cannot verify or falsify its situation.

LEFT: The **CHINESE ROOM** was proposed by John Searle in 1980. A person who does not speak Chinese is given instructions that enable them to respond to written Chinese questions with appropriate answers. Searle argues that this person does not truly know the language, despite appearing to do so, and that simply processing symbols does not equate to true understanding.

RIGHT: The **CHINA BRAIN**: In 1978 Ned Block imagined the people of China gathered at the imperial palace, each with a radio and instructions corresponding to the behaviour of a single neuron. Since there are approx. 85 billion neurons in the brain, if everyone follows their instructions, would this organisation have degree of consciousness?

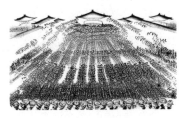

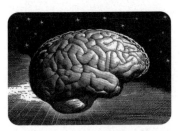

LEFT: **BOLTZMAN BRAINS**: There is a possibility that a disembodied brain could coalesce from random space dust by chance. What if it formed complete with memories, like a snapshot of a person possessing the perfect illusion of being real? How then could it know if its memories were all false, or if it had actually lived those moments?

RIGHT: **BRAIN IN A VAT**: In 1973 Gilbert Harman imagined this scenario: A scientist puts your brain in a vat and connects wires to simulate the world perfectly. From outside it seems a grotesque experiment; but inside you experience a normal life. Is there any way we can know if we are a brain in a vat? If not, can we be confident that anything is real?

KNOWING & EXPERIENCE
spectrum speculations

Mary is a prisoner in a totalitarian state which has banned all colour. As a result, she has lived her whole life entirely in black and white. She has read all about colour, the neuroscience of colour perception and the physics of the visible light spectrum (*below*). In fact Mary is an expert on colour like no other—but, and this is the crux—if she left her cell and *actually* saw colour, would she learn something new?

If she does, then that suggests knowledge about the physical world is inexhaustive: even knowing all there is to know, without experience Mary lacks something. If she doesn't, then it would appear the idea of a subjective experiential realm outside the physical is wrong.

Such thought experiments raise unsettling questions. Can I ever know 'what it is like' to be you? I may know your likes, dislikes, fears, hopes and dreams: but do I truly know what it is to be in your shoes? If I was to share your head for a day would I learn something new?

These questions are explored by *phenomenology,* a philosophy of conscious experience. Phenomenologists argue that we can never know what it is like to be someone else because we'll never have their exact memories, history, body, brain—and if we did, we wouldn't merely know what it is like to be them, we would *be them* (*opposite top*). For phenomenologists, all empathy is imperfect; but equally, all forms of communication a miracle.

ABOVE: **WHAT IS IT LIKE TO BE A BAT**: In 1974 Thomas Nagel described some bat scientists who know everything about bats, how they fly, eat, navigate, behave and have even mapped their complete brain states. Nagel then asked: "Do these scientists actually know what it is like to BE a bat? Or if we turned them into bats for an hour, would they learn something new?"

ABOVE: **PHILOSOPHICAL ZOMBIES**: P-zombies are identical to conscious humans but lack an inner mental life. Assuming p-zombies respond to stimuli and talk about their experiences as if they were conscious, is it possible to distinguish them from real humans? This thought experiment explores the hard problem of consciousness which explores the difficulty of explaining how and why we have subjective experiences, or qualia, arising from our physical brain processes.

ABOVE: **THE MISSING HUE**: philosopher David Hume [1711 – 1776] considered a spectrum of blue with a gap between the shades. Could a person imagine what ought to go there? And if so, does that mean some knowledge derives from outside of empirical experience?

FACING PAGE: **COLOUR CONSCIOUS**: Mary has only seen black and white, but has a deep knowledge about colour. Without direct experience, however, can her knowledge be complete?

GALILEO & NEWTON
imaginary drops and shots

You may know of Galileo's experiment where he dropped two balls of different weights off the Leaning Tower of Pisa to show all objects fall at the same rate, but did you realise it never happened? Or at least not in physical space—Galileo carried out the whole thing in his head.

In his book *On Motion*, Galileo Galilei [1564–1642] imagined two objects, one heavier than the other, connected by a string. He then dropped them from a height: if heavy objects fall faster than lighter ones, then the lighter object should pull the string taught and slow the heavier object. If we consider the whole thing however, its mass is greater than the heavier object by itself, and thus should fall faster, leading to a contradiction. Galileo brilliantly concluded Aristotle's theory of heavier objects falling faster must be false.

Isaac Newton [1642–1727] also used thought experiments. To model orbital motion he imagined firing a cannonball from a mountain top. Newton reasoned that although the ball still falls towards the Earth's centre, if the speed it travels is exactly right, the height it falls is matched by the curvature of the planet, and thus it would enter a stable orbit (*opposite, lower*). Using this straightforward thought experiment, Newton posited that gravity was both universal and the key to the motion of all planetary bodies.

LEFT: **KANT'S ORBITS**: In 1747 the philosopher Immanuel Kant commented that it is the three-dimensional nature of space that gives rise to the inverse square law with respect to gravity. Later scientists have noticed that if space was four-dimensional then the forces would obey an inverse cube law, and most orbits (except for near circular ones) would be unstable. How convenient for us, that space is three dimensional!

RIGHT: **NEWTON'S CANNONBALL**: Issac Newton used the following thought experiment to think about orbits. If a cannonball is fired at a normal speed from a mountain top, it will be pulled down by gravity and fall to Earth. If it is fired at huge velocity then it will escape gravity and fly into space. However, fired at just the right speed, the cannonball will orbit the Earth at a constant distance from the surface.

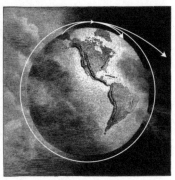

FACING PAGE: **GALILEO'S DROP**:
Two objects of different weight are strung together and dropped: if heavy objects fall faster, the lighter object should pull on the string, slowing the heavier one. But both fall at the same rate under gravity.
LEFT: During the Apollo 15 moon mission an astronaut actually dropped a hammer and a feather that landed simultaneously, proving Galileo's hunch that gravitational acceleration is not dependant on mass.

EINSTEIN'S IMAGINATION
thinking at lightspeed

Albert Einstein [1879–1955] created many thought experiments. His earliest imagined chasing a light beam at the speed of light—the beam would appear at rest, though oscillating: a seeming impossibility. A later one teases out the idea of special relativity. A photon of light is bounced from a mirror on the floor of a moving train to another mirror on the ceiling (*below*). An observer on the train sees the light travel distance d in time t but an observer on the platform sees the light travel a greater distance d' in time t'. But the speed of light is constant. So time must be passing at different rates for the two observers.

Einstein's theory of general relativity was also preceded by a thought experiment. He asked us to imagine a man falling in a box at a constant rate: if the man dropped objects in the box they would 'float' as if weightless. If the box was constantly accelerated, everything would be pushed to one end of the box consistent with being in a uniform gravitational field. There is no experiment the man could do to verify whether he was in such a field or if the box was accelerating. Thus, the seeds for the equivalency principle, in which gravitational and inertial mass are equivalent, were planted in an entirely imaginary world.

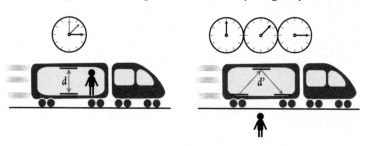

ABOVE: **EINSTEIN'S ELEVATOR**: 1. *A person inside a stationary sealed elevator being pulled down by gravity would* 2. *feel the same as if they were accelerating upwards at a constant rate.* 3. *Conversely an elevator in freefall would* 4. *feel the same as if it were floating in space.*

ABOVE: The **TWIN PARADOX** highlights the strange effects of general relativity by imagining identical twins. 1. One stays on Earth, the other 2. speeds off to a nearby star at close to light speed. Due to relativistic time dilation, the traveling twin experiences less time than the stationary one, so 3. when she returns, the traveller is younger than her stay at home sister.

ABOVE: A **TRAIN** and a **TUNNEL** are the same length when at rest relative to each other. The train accelerates to close to light speed, experiencing relativistic length dilation. 1. From Amy's perspective aboard the train, it is the tunnel in motion and experiencing length dilation, so it seems impossible for the train to fit in the tunnel. 2. However from Bob's perspective at rest nearby, the train appears to get shorter and fits easily in the tunnel. Both Amy and Bob are correct in their own reference frames, but see the situation differently due to their relative motion.

SCHRÖDINGER'S CAT
and other quantum weirdness

According to quantum mechanics, it is possible for unobserved objects to exist in multiple states—light can be both a particle and a wave, and electrons can be spinning both 'up' and 'down' at the same time. This is known as *quantum superposition* and, using probabilities, the chances for an object to be in one of its various states can be modelled without definitively saying which state the object is in. This is comfortable at the tiny scales quantum objects exist in but at larger sizes it can appear bizarre: it would be like flipping a coin, hiding the result, and saying it was both heads *and* tails simultaneously.

Erwin Schrödinger [1887–1961] constructed a thought experiment to illustrate just how strange quantum mechanics is. He imagined a cat in a sealed box (*below*). A vial of deadly chemicals is placed inside it which cracks open if some quantum system is in a certain state—say, a radioactive element decaying rather than not decaying. If the vial breaks the cat dies, otherwise the cat lives. But, following the logic of quantum superposition, while the box remains closed and we cannot see inside, then the radioactive element is both decayed and not decayed, modelled using a probability distribution. So the vial of poison must be simultaneously broken and whole, and the cat must also both be dead and alive!

1.   2.   3.

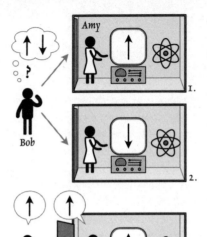

Amy is in a lab looking at a quantum effect (eg, electron spin) while Bob waits outside. Amy measures the electron, collapsing its wavefunction (as spin up). Bob is unaware of this result, and, until Amy tells him, he has to model both of the lab's two possible quantum states:

1. Amy finds the electron is spin up.
2. Amy finds the electron is spin down.

At this point, they disagree: Amy says the electron is spin up, but Bob says its wavefunction is uncollapsed.

3. Eventually, Bob learns of Amy's result. But at what point did the laboratory's wavefunction collapse—when Amy measured the electron, or when she informed Bob?

ABOVE: THE LOVE PARADOX: In the Many Worlds interpretation of quantum physics, parallel universes are created for each choice we make. 1. In this world you meet your true love in a bar, whilst 2. in a parallel universe you never meet each other.

ABOVE: THE QBIST PARADOX: In QBism, an interpretation of quantum physics which allows for different observer realities, Jane may see fairies—they may be real in her universe—while for Bob they are just nonsense, and he never sees any.

WHEELER'S CHOICES
can the present affect the past?

The DELAYED CHOICE is a thought experiment designed by physicist John Archibald Wheeler [1911–2008] to investigate the nature of wave-particle duality in quantum mechanics. Photons are sent through a double-slit and their behaviour recorded on a screen. Left to itself, an interference pattern appears, indicating that photons behave as waves (*below left*). However, if detectors are used to determine which slit any photon passes through, then the interference pattern disappears and the photons seem to behave like particles (*below right and opposite top*).

Wheeler introduced his delay by placing the detectors *after* the photons had already passed through the slits (*opposite centre*). Surprisingly, the interference pattern once again disappeared, as if the photons 'knew' they were going to be observed, and had changed their behaviour accordingly in the past. Wheeler then introduced a further step. If a scrubber was added to the setup which destroyed the information about which slits the photons had passed through, then the interference pattern reappeared, as if the photons were once again confident that no-one was looking. Wheeler designed the experiment in 1983, but it was not until 2007, 2011 and 2016 that it was proven to be correct.

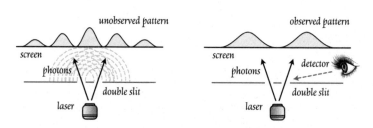

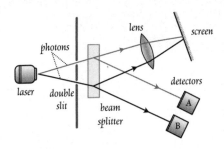

LEFT: **PART 1–THE DOUBLE SLIT:**
Photons are sent through a double-slit onto a screen. When unobserved, an interference pattern appears, showing the photons behave as waves. However, when detectors (A & B) are used to determine which slit a photon passes through, the interference pattern disappears, and the photons behave as particles.

RIGHT: **PART 2–THE DELAYED CHOICE:**
Wheeler then introduced a delay by placing the detectors after the photons had already reached the screen (C & D). Once again the pattern disappeared if the photons were observed. However, if the detectors were configured to remove any identifying information (E & F) the interference pattern reappeared, as if the photons 'knew' they were unobserved.

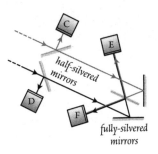

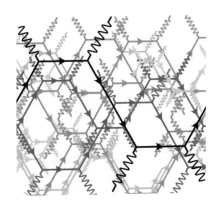

LEFT: **JUST ONE ELECTRON:**
Wheeler suggested that the entire universe might be made up of a single electron moving forwards and backwards in time. Although the thought experiment itself was not taken seriously, it did inspire the crucial insight that anti-electrons (positrons) could be viewed as equivalent to electrons travelling backwards through time.

SUSSKIND'S ELEPHANT
holes and horizons

The idea of a dark star so massive that even light could not escape was first proposed by astronomical pioneer John Michell [1724–1793]. Since then, the existence of *black holes* has pushed scientific understanding to its limits, and physicists have developed a number of thought experiments to get to grips with the complexities.

In the early 1990s, Leonard Susskind came up with a surreal thought experiment about what happens at a black hole's event horizon. He imagined an unfortunate elephant falling into a black hole. From the elephant's perspective, it merely crosses the horizon and enters the black hole. But from the point of view of a safe observer, watching from afar, the elephant appears to be in serious trouble (*see examples opposite*). Susskind's resolution to this paradox is to say that both realities are true, one for the elephant, one for the observer, and since neither can communicate with the other, there's no contradiction.

In another related thought experiment, Susskind realised that, weirdly, a full description of any volume of space can be described on a lower dimensional surface (*right*).

In a similar way, it can be said that the boundary between thought experiments and the conceptual leaps and calculations of theoretical physics is a blurry one indeed.

LEFT: The **BLACK HOLE INFORMATION PARADOX** arises from an apparent conflict between the principles of quantum mechanics and general relativity regarding the fate of information falling into a black hole. General relativity states that the information should be lost forever, whereas quantum mechanics demands that the information must be preserved.

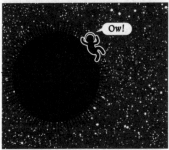

LEFT: The **FIREWALL PARADOX** imagines an observer falling into a black hole and being incinerated by high-energy particles at the event horizon. The paradox arises between the no-hair theorem, which implies that any object that crosses the event horizon would be indistinguishable from any other, and quantum entanglement, which suggests that particles have a special connection even when separated by great distances.

LEFT: **SUSSKIND'S ELEPHANT**: Imagine an elephant falling into a black hole. The elephant simply experiences crossing the event horizon. However, a safer observer sees the elephant fizzing on the edge of the horizon. Susskind's resolution involves complementarity: either we describe the situation beyond the horizon OR the radiation that comes out—no observer can see both.

FACING PAGE: **THE HOLOGRAPHIC PRINCIPLE** says that all the information needed to fully describe a 3D region of space—all the galaxies, stars, planets and brains inside it—can be fully encoded on the 2D surface of its enclosing sphere.

WHAT CAN BE KNOWN?
the limits of conscious knowledge

The outside world is complex, confusing, and often unknowable. Conversely, we have mastery of our inner world: nothing is hidden, and you cannot be mistaken about whether you hold your own beliefs. Or can you? Amia Srnivasan argues that we sometimes lack knowledge about our own conscious experience.

Imagine daydreaming of a romantic interest. Slowly change elements to make them less attractive—slightly more demanding, less reliable, more annoying—and reflect on whether you are still attracted. Is it possible to make a mistake? The argument goes as follows. After each tiny change, you will continue to believe you are attracted. This is only natural because, as Srnivasan noted in 2013, [We] *don't just believe at random. Our mental lives are structured by certain dispositions. When we believe something in one set of circumstances, in very similar circumstances we have a disposition to believe the same thing.* Nonetheless, eventually a change will remove your attraction but you will continue to believe you are still attracted, now mistakenly.

Most concerningly, this reasoning can apply to any conscious experience: feeling cold, hungry, scared, relaxed or angry. Important or trivial, we are vulnerable to making mistakes about our inner world. You may believe you love (or hate) someone, but in reality small changes in circumstances have altered your conscious experience: nevertheless you continue to believe in error.

ABOVE: *A gradually heated frog is unaware of the incremental change.*

58